CW00859067

READ BY MOONLIGHT

READ BY MOONLIGHT

RAMONA JUDE

Library of Congress Control Number:		2018913464
ISBN:	Hardcover	978-1-9845-6535-8
	Softcover	978-1-9845-6534-1
	eBook	978-1-9845-6533-4

Print information available on the last page.

Rev. date: 11/09/2018

To order additional copies of this book, contact:
Xlibris
1-888-795-4274
www.Xlibris.com
Orders@Xlibris.com
784757

THE POEM ABOUT THE POET

A poet goes golfing
Which is weird for the poet as she purposefully
put herself in a place of white, old men
Which is the epitome of hell, if you've read her poems
But it's alone, and quiet
Like she is now since he left

A poet eats her dinner alone
Which is supposed to be radical and progressive since she needs no man
But this was his favorite table
Where their favorite story stemmed from

A poet goes dancing with her friends to show
she can still move like the ocean
The curves of her body pulling and stretching like the tides with every twist
And she proves she is still a roadside flower
Unknown to the common man, But still beautiful, still wild
Growing in places where she wasn't meant to grow

A poet goes to write
But cannot for there's no one to read it to
There's no one to critique it anymore
It's just a poet in her apartment, writing at a desk Because at the
end of the day, she's just a poet No longer is anyone's home

A poet goes shopping
And feels naked trying on clothes
Because her body feels cold and unfamiliar
Without him wrapped around it,
Without him to tell her she looks beautiful
The poet feels naked
Without him

MOONLIT RIDE

$83.56
That's how much I spent on gas about 4 hours
ago when I first got in my car
But this is my 6th trip this month
Meaning, I've really dumped about $500 in my tank for trips like these

Sometimes, when it's just the stars who hear me struggle to fall asleep
And the moon watches me toss and turn for
hours before I decide to hop in my car
I plan trips with no destination
No one to visit
No planned pit stops
It's just driving

While the routes are always different and the lengths of trips vary
I carry out the same ritualistic routine out nearly every time I've
become not only a create of habit, but also nocturnal Making
me an owl or bat while most are canaries or egrets

I start off by just sitting and staring at my steering wheel
My old friend
Always reliable, always comforting
Truly a sight for sore, tired eyes

I then turn on my music Because while I'll press shuffle
I still know the order by heart It's all soul music
Trips like these are meant for three people: Me, driving
My subconscious, riding backseat driver
My soul, sitting shotgun right next to me
We pick up Otis Redding, Etta James, and Janis Joplin along the way
Sometimes, my lost hopes and broken dreams slam
into my windshield next to the lightning bugs

I can see them, and I can't scrape them off with my windshield wipers
All I can do is try not to let them distract me or stare at them for too long

It's after the music starts to all sound the same and the
stars stop looking like rare jewels and more like dust
specks that my thoughts roll in like storm clouds
They're loud like thunder
As blinding and vivid as lightning
And as impactful as golf ball sized hail

I'll think about the poems I'll never write
Like how in love or happy I am
Because those feelings may engulf you and be so powerful
that they will recalibrate your moral compass to the
point where your north is no longer true north
But that doesn't mean they will last forever
Words are forever
The black and white of scripture is permanent
It's the same reason I won't write about sadness or loneliness
They won't last long for a reason
So i won't put them on a page where they'll
become fixtures of my work and my mind

I think about all the people who are up at this god forsaken hour
The men and women who single out others for money Who get people's
loose change to pay for their next meal Who devote their days to sleeping
Because no one attacks the homeless in the light
But when the darkness of night masks people's morals and dignity
That's an entirely different story

Couples in love are up too
Fooled into thinking they don't have every day of the rest of their
lives with each other That every moment could be the one they
think about when they take their final breath Waiting on the other
side for the person they spent all their nights staying awake for

I usually pull into my driveway right when the
moon pulls into his resting place
I lay down and let my eyelids pull over my eyes
as the sunshine pulls over the Earth
These trips are good for the soul
And sometimes, I can't help but think my mind keeps
itself up so that I'll take trips like these

OPTIONS

The way I see it
In this world
You are one thing or another
There's thousands of colors that fall upon the chromatic
spectrum but people are black and white
This world and the challenges it presents are either overcame
Or overcome the challenger

You either get a career or you get a job
A job is something you do to get paid
It's something you do to make sure you can get by
A job is usually the type of work in which people look through you like
some mythical mist that is barely noticeable in the scheme of other's lives
But you are able to see if the mist had invaded
the room if you squint your eyes enough
It's your bellhop
Your secretary
Your waitress that serves you breakfast every other thursday that
has three sons that you will never ask how they are doing
All workers who have families and plights and beautiful
life stories that you'll never care to hear about
A job, most of all, is a pit stop
Just a spectacle on the side of the road on your
way to getting where you're going

A career is something you work your whole life for
Is something you do to provide not only for your family
But for your need to contribute to the society that got you
here today A career is something that makes you want
to get up in the morning It's part of your purpose
Its part of the reason why you're here

A career is something you can look back on
25 years after the first day and say
"I did it, I did everything I was made to do"

You see, you're either a wife, or you're a girlfriend
When you're the girlfriend, you meet the family once at something
big enough to where people notice you're there, but don't catch
your name because you're not going to stick around anyways
When you're the girlfriend, you spend the night You're not cut out
to leave a toothbrush there Bring your cactus to their place
Put your shoes anywhere besides next to the door because the connection
forged between you two is something composed of rubber bands
It'll hold you together for a short time before it
snaps and hurts both of you upon recoil

When you're the wife, you watch the third cousin while the second cousin,
the aunt, and the love of your life go out to buy shelves for your new place
This is because you moved into the family
Taken in like a puppy at a pet store on main street with a front window
big enough to see her ridiculously huge sea blue eyes as you drive by
When you're the wife, you don't worry about the exes you never met
The coworkers you don't see but hear about everyday
The friends from high school they used to call
and talk through every night with
Because you are he one in their life that's going to love them every day
Pick them up when they trip so they don't even get the chance to fall down
And be the one person who says their name
with no malevolent hidden intentions

You're either a mother or a birthgiver
A birth giver has sons and daughters, but does not raise them
But rather, brings them into a world that will teach them everything
they need to know to survive but also shows them that they
don't need anyone or anything because if their own other
The sole reason they're alive doesn't want them or love them
Then who is going to?

8

A birth giver provides food and money
Gives a roof to sleep under
A bed to report to at night
But doesn't give you faith that you'll always be loved no
matter what happens in the course of their life
Doesn't give you a sense of security that you'll
forever have a home to go to

A mother loves her kids with unshakeable commitment and kindness
Even if her children are not of her own bloodline
A mother builds a home out of sticks and leaves under an
overpass when her and her family get evicted from their house
She bounds the sticks together with stories of girls with long
blonde hair and boys who make everything in the city okay
so that the kids know that everything will be okay
That no monster that the mother speaks of being slain in her
tales will never hurt them because their mother is there
And nothing can harm them so long as their mother is there

See, there are always two types of people There's those who work and
those who dream There's those who breathe and those who live And
there's those who understood this poem And those who never will

PATRON SAINTS

St. Anthony is the patron saint of lost things While raised Greek
and in the Catholic Church I was raised on superstitions
So, spilled salt always was tossed over my left shoulder
And I thank St. Tony himself when I find my car keys after 3 hours

When I was sick
I prayed to Saint Raphael
No dosage of Nyquil could surmount to the amount of
faith I had in some obscure white man that died long
before I was scared to put my shoes on a bed
Or before Sunday school loomed over kids heads
like the storms produced by Saint Barbara

I would look to the skies through stained glass windows to
see lightning bolts just kiss the surface of the Earth
Leaving the Earth to want more
No matter how bad each strike hurt the blessed ground
And I'd close my eyes and listen to the pitter patter of raindrops that
fell so delicately and so strategically placed by Barbie herself
Along with the rain came the thunder that silenced the skies
And the lightning that brought it back to life

When I fell in love
I prayed to Saint Valentine that this was real
That this wasn't some temporary blessing
Or short term allegory used to teach others a lesson through example
Or some sick joke from whatever deity I pissed off that day
I prayed to Saint Christopher to bless the ground I walked on
The bed I dreamt in
The car I drove
Because I needed good fortune and to be
drenched in holy water and blessings

I didn't want to pray to Saint Anthony to bring back
another person I had loved and lost again
I didn't want to reread hymns about finding comfort in solitude
Because being alone isn't sitting by yourself in a dark
room At least in the dark room you know that it's just you
Loneliness is a curse stricken by the big man himself
It's sitting in the back pew with no one beside you
Screaming the songs dedicated to God's favorite
workers to make sure you're heard
But doing it while also watching families with 6 kids and old
women who have been friends since high school and never
left their hometowns and that one pregnant couple that lives 3
blocks down between the laundromat and the grocery store
While none of them look back
Because why would they?

I squeak out a note for Saint Cecilia
Hoping this high E flat isn't killing her like this old wood bench is killing me
And as I walk through the front doors
I say a quick thank you to Saint Monica
Because at least I made it another Sunday

SANITORIUM

"Did you see her just start crying in class? It's like she's
depressed or something" "Oh my god, oh my god, I'm
going to get fired! My anxiety is through the roof!"
"I swear I never see him come to lunch"

Marilyn Monroe died in a room peppered with
beautiful pearl colored pills made just for her
She was born with one name
Died with another
But lived with a monster that never changed names
Just changed form in accordance to the person it stalked
Depression plagued the star along with everlasting fame and eternal glory
Going down in history as the woman to be
Because she was beautiful
Because she was sought after by all Because she
was a triple threat Because she was Marilyn
Not because she cried exclusively behind closed doors
And fought demons insurmountable to most
And dedicated her being to making others value the lives
they lived through admiring her on the silver screen

Elton John dragged his bejeweled digits across keys of black
and white and made the glory days what they were
Glorious
And after the show After the roar subsided After the fourth encore
He'd waltz to his dressing room
One, two, three Take off his rings Four, five, six
Examine the fingers that just got done making
thousands of dollars in one night

Two, two, three
And tickle his throat with the same fingers
that tickled keys just moments ago
Four, five, six
And empty everything he forced himself to swallow that day
Three, two, three
From the same cavity that could belt notes that would make men
and women give in to emotions they didn't even know they had
Four, five, six
Bulimia consumed Mr. John's mind like glitter consumed
the eyes of anyone that went to his show

Nina Simone never missed a beat and sang with such soul
It would push, pull, and rock her followers to
their very core with every note
She would get off stage after singing about feeling good
knowing full well she was more of a pipe bomb
Ready to go off and create mass destruction at any time
Bipolar disorder, that's what they call it
The thing that made the queen of soul more like a string
puppet Controlled by something that constantly loomed over
her head Pulling her in different directions with no patterns
No predictable next move
No consistency

The Mouse, the Princesses, the Magic
Walt Disney made it his life's work to make children blush
and laugh until their cheeks hurt and their dimples became
ornaments on faces young and old everywhere
This is years after he grew up without a laugh
Without a smile
Seeing knuckles to his face way more frequently than joy
Connecting his body to a belt long before he connected to an audience
Mr. Disney Cartoon pioneer Abuse survivor

She lead one of the most powerful nations
with astonishing beauty and grace
Leading those to believe that when she removed her crown
She was done seeing thrones for the day
For after spending days upon a cushioned seat
Sat upon by her ancestors who ruled with the
same undeniable power as her
Princess Diana would spend her nights bent over a porcelain throne
With the bulimia beast holding her hair back

Michelangelo, autism
JK Rowling, depression
Vincent van Gogh, bipolar disorder Mary Todd Lincoln, schizophrenia
Winston Churchill, depression Carrie Fisher, anxiety
Leonardo da Vinci, dyslexia
Edgar Allan Poe, alcoholism
Charles Darwin, obsessive compulsive disorder
Buzz Aldrin, depression
Ozzy Osbourne, bipolar disorder
King George VI, developmental trauma disorder The girl having a
panic attack in the library Future president of the United States
The boy that you sit next to on the bus who pukes
over and over again through the night
Grammy award recipient in 6 years
The girl slicing and dicing her wrist like it's melted butter
The leading researcher to the cure of Alzheimer's in 9 years
The boy avoiding the cafeteria at any and all costs
Gold medal winner in speed skating in the next Olympics
The girl washing her hands until the white suds turn pink then red
Future author of the next American classic novel

Success takes crazy
Insanity fuels drive
The world would not turn if it were not for those
who dared to venture to the far ends of the
Earth knowing that the world really wasn't flat
Those same psychopaths The same societal
rejects With the same lack of sanity
Keep life as interesting as it is
Because an illness of the mind isn't the end of the world
It just makes you a better success story

THE EXPLANATION

See, you were not a ghost, or a spirit, or an apparition
Something so black and white, so simple, does not fit what you were
Being a phantom is too easy to fathom for your kind of intricacy

You were a box of sugary cereal I loved as a child:
Something I loved so dearly when I was too young to understand
how detrimental, how truly horrific and maleficent you were,
But when I'm 18 and alone, truly independent, for the first time
I'll wander the aisles looking for you

But even the dimmest of minds knows that a box of cereal can't just
disappear, which is what makes you the white floaty things in my eye
Something I'd see for a fraction of a second but would disappear too
quickly for me to catch you, or truly look at you, or try to talk to you
Leaving you to be a distant memory at best,
a constant teasing sight at worst

But even the simplest of people get that a spot in my eye is
too close for something of your kind of nothingness
Therefore, you're more so the moon
Not just any moon, but the moon I'd watch on car rides home
Close enough to catch a glimpse of, but too far to hug, to love, to feel
And everytime you came into focus, I'd think "he'll surely
come home this time, he has to come inside this time",
but of course you never did

But that's because a lion cannot come inside any house,
of course. Something so loud, so destructive,
something meant to be feared, not loved, do not belong in homes,
they belong amongst the other beasts who do
not care to look after their own kin

While I grew up wanting to be a ballerina, along with every other
little girl in the world, I think I was meant for something else
Maybe a chef, as I spent so much time in grocery stores,
in markets, in superstores, hoping your stupid, one-of-a-
kind, show up for a short time brand would be there

Or possibly, an optometrist. After all, I've spent so much
time looking into so many eyes, so many souls,
to see if the same white spots, the same pain, the
same questions, the same absence are there
But I just ended wanting to be blind by the end of it all
Even better, I could become an astronomer!
I did spend too much time with my head in the clouds,
naively thinking you would come home some day
but that's only because the stars told me so when I begged the
moon to show itself for more than a small fraction of our time

I know what I could never be, I could never be a father
Because your mastery of a disappearing act, your sour taste,
your lack of duty,
is a jack of trades I don't care to learn

THE FUNERAL

I went to a funeral today
But it was the oddest funeral I think I'll ever have the pleasure of going to

The casket held no body
But it held countless memories, piles of pictures, and tons of tears
And to my surprise,
The further down the casket I looked, The more and more empty it looked
As if the deceased was worth saving the least at the end

The flowers, oh the flowers
How dead they were!
It was a sweet collection of 6 bouquets
2 valentines days, 2 birthdays, 2 anniversary arrangements
But of course, you never get fresh flowers for something
that's been dead for quite a while now
So really, they were the most appropriate funeral flowers I've ever seen

And the color scheme, how peculiar the palette was
It was blue, but a special kind of blue
Not too light, but that special kind of blue
right after the sunrise turns to day
This color was only described to me once by someone who's name is
only found at the bottom of glasses and the butts of smoking things
The beginning of something blue was paired up
with a red, but a special kind of red

Not too violent, but that special kind of red right
when the day ends and the stars and the moon meet
once again, after being separated for so long
The end of something red and beginning something blue were
so beautiful together, and quite frankly really set the mood

The only thing that was truly particular was the sight of the death
It was in a restaurant on a cloudy day when the most beautiful
thing I've ever seen was killed in a matter of minutes
And embarrassingly enough, I didn't think a murder took
place until i saw the killer walk through the door
Continuing on with his life, as if he didn't just end something so
full of potential, so full of life, so full of things left unsaid
As I sat there, with the remaining pieces of whatever
was left in my hands, I started planning the wake
The grieving
The funeral
The crying, the crying, the crying

And I thank you, dearly beloved, for being gathered here today
To pay your respects
And we ask you to please, leave the box of possessions at the door
Management will be around to collect the memories
and miscellaneous items when I can

THE GREAT WAR

Did you know that the Syrian conflict has produced the largest mass of
refugees and displaced people in Europe since the second World War?
And I walk down the street thinking of this
Towards the apartment with two bedrooms and
my mother's name on the front door
I feel sand between my toes
I hear arabic between my ears
And I see my apartment building sitting snug between
the French Alps and the German Alps

I wake up every morning in a bed that smells like my
sweat and homes my 12 pound cat in the corner
But this isn't my bed
It feels like a cot
Just a temporary place to sleep while I try to find my way home
As I lay in my cot
I think of those I lost in my own war
My brother, who I haven't seen in a year after he left the camp to
fight his own war and demons that whisper his name in his ear
My other brother, who doesn't know my name or that we share a father
My mother, whose eyes constantly see dead loved ones
Whose ears hear bombshells explode forever and beyond all finite time
Whose hands are red from washing away the memories
she had of the man that started this war
Whose tongue tastes nothing as she starves to be happy
As she feens for a home to go back to
As she craves the good old days before the war

When I lay in the cool desert sand
And look up at the sky
Thinking of how free the constellations are
How the war will never truly end
How the war has technically been over since
the dictator finally left for good
How he landed airstrikes along my cheekbone With
every knuckle connecting at a different time But just
close enough to forge mass destruction
And the sounds of bombs coming down on buildings that
would soon thereafter crumble could not come close
to causing the amount of damage his voice did
At least his voice came before the airstrikes rained down
Warning of inevitable danger
Of unpreventable death

I get up from the san and run to a mosque to pray
As I take off towards the holy safe haven
And my lungs begin to burn like the pretty little cigarettes
I down to cope with the tax the war has put on me
I think again of those I watched perish in battle
The old little girl I once loved and knew so dearly
who thought all humans were goof
That no one was capable of enough evil to
intentionally bring harm onto others
The dream I had set up for myself passed too
My family I pictured having vanished
The strong woman I thought I'd become crumbled
before me like the country's morals did
I heard my faith in others get blasted to bit from a mile away
For the man that homed half my DNA was the first to set me in his
scope and attempt to take his shot from across the battlefield

I watch on the news how boats of children
succumbed to the restless tides of the sea
I witnessed the millions of atoms of hydrogen and
oxygen swallowed the babies up whole
WIthout a regret
Without a hesitation
I saw that they never made it to safety
They never had the chance to, let alone a chance at a full, happy life
At least I crawled through the deep snow in the mountains
of Switzerland to make it back to the apartment on the
second floor of the brick building I call home
But the war will never be over
I think of this as i drag my feet that are weighed
down by boots up the stairs
The war will never be won by one side
Someone will just fall out of sight of the other's shot
Someone will just slip up
And isn't it beautiful how simple that is compared to the war itself?

THE PEST POEM

Oh Mr. Bug
Mr. Bug on a rug
Mr. Bug on a rug inside my house
I'm killing you now because i need to save you
I don't want you to see what it's like outside this house
I'm the best home you'll have anyways

Oh. Miss Mouse
Miss. Mouse in my house on Main Street
I trapped you for your own good
People get snatched on Main Street, don't you
know? And with what you're wearing?
I just don't want to see you get hurt

Oh little ladybug
Little ladybug with 9 dots
Little ladybug with 9 dots under my shoe
Don't you know what other humans would do to you? They
might brush you away or put you under a glass
I promise i wont squash you again
I promise it was a one time thing
I promise I love you
You know I squished you because I love you, don't you?

C'mon crazy caterpillar
Crazy caterpillar on a leaf
Did you think you could really leave your leaf and me?
Don't you know you won't find another me?
Don't you know I know where your parents live?
Don't you know I will always find you?
Don't you know you can't leave?

Hey now, bespotted bullfrog
Bespotted bullfrog with the beautiful ballads
You have such a powerful voice
If you didn't want me to do that, why didn't you use that
pretty little voice of yours? Why didn't you say no?
No, why didn't you really say no?
Why are you acting like you didn't want me? I know you want me
I know no knows that it really means yes
I know you really meant yes

You know what really bugs me?
How much the sun burns my insecticide drenched skin Since your poison
tipped tongue tried to clip my wings Tried to cut my dreams short
Tried to trap me from escaping your slimy hands

I think I might move to the desert
The strongest bugs live there so really, it's where i belong Plus i
have never met an exterminator from down south So adios senor
I have a migration I can't miss

THE WORLD'S HAIRIEST SHRINK

Wednesdays are my favorite day of the week
Not because that's when my favorite murder mystery updates
But because that's the day I get to see the
best therapist known to mankind
He's not licensed, he's not trained
He doesn't even talk
But he does prefer salmon soft food over chicken

He prances around the office as if he's king of the jungle
Ruling over his 6 foot carpeted tower and vast forest of
catnip with dignity and respect for almost all
He has no degree hung upon his wall
But rather, a cast collection of moths, flies, and gnats
who met their final landing on my therapist's wall

My shrink cannot hand me any tissues when I weep
Because he lacks opposable thumbs
But not sympathy
For when my waterworks start to flow
And I drown my hands in tears and sorrows
My therapist does not hesitate to come dry my face
with his whiskers and already wet nose

My psychologist launches himself into my lap
And I look closely at his paws
Making sure to take note of his nubs on his paws that
look remarkably similar to the pills I'm prescribed to make
sure I wake up the morning after I take them
And every morning after that

Thank god for my Wednesdays and my therapist
Because without them
I wouldn't be here today
And if I wasn't here today
Then who would feed my therapist?

YOU'VE BEEN SERVED

I'm a waitress with law school dreams
Living two lives in one head
Dreaming of defending paupers while serving cheap food to princes

While my feet ache waiting tables for more hours than I have toes
I think of the aching hearts of mothers I will one day promise to heal
We will fight for a new life, away from the danger
of abusive husbands or boyfriends
And I will fight for their right to freedom someday I think to
myself as I dump a half eaten burger into the trash can

While I balance 6 plates between both arms,
I think of how I'll balance true facts and a little bit of theatrics to impress
a jury so well, I'll get unanimous verdicts in my favor every time

While I shout out orders that I've been waiting on for 45 minutes,
I think of the shouts that workers scream in protests day in and day out
Begging for fair pay and equality in their workplaces
Which, mind you, I'll have no problem fighting for with
impeccable focus and unbreakable determination

While I spurt rapid italian at the grill chef from Sicily in the back
I imagine how priceless it will be when I read
immigrants from all over the globe
Who have battled and sacrificed more than their lives to get here
Their rights for the first time as US citizens

While I roll forks and knives into white scrolls of 25 cent napkins
I think of the hours I'll spend in my firm
Sharpening each case with so many facts and gutsy presentation tactics
It'll be as dangerous as staring a gun down it's barrel
I'll be as intimidating as being face to face
with a sword when I take the floor
With my opposition fearing how I might pick apart any story or allegation

When I get in my car
Both my car and myself reeking of oil
Saying a plethora of prayers to get my heap of metal to start
I think of how I won't need a car to get home
to my beautiful penthouse in the city
And how my office will always smell of happiness
As my grease slathered dreams had finally come true

And when I stand on my tip toes to drop my
$2.53 in tips in my beloved tip jar
My body stretching like a white lie stretches reality to
add, I stare deep into my pitiful pile of money
I remember to keep my head up
For my plights will be over soon and that any day is a good day
to go to law school with a dream and a tuition paid in tips

5 THINGS I NOTICED
WHEN I SAW YOU AGAIN

1. You got your hair cut
   How easy the scissors must have glided through your
   curly brown hair in comparison to the piercing of an
   ice pick i felt when the day hell froze over came
   When our red hot love went cold after sitting out for too long
   And you left to go cool off

2. You shook no man's hand in the room
   Which truly highlights how infantile you are
   Maybe you didn't shake anyone's hand because you couldn't reach
   Since you still need to grow up

3. You ate not one, but two plates of food
   And while I used to find this adorable, it actually
   shows how much of a sinner you are
   Gluttony, for not only food, but for the taste
   of other women in your mouth
   Sloth, for being too lazy to let yourself fully commit to a woman
   who you once claimed to love more than the world itself
   Who you used to slow dance with at 3 am in your
   kitchen while she wore one of your old shirts
   Just to study her movements
   Get her steps down just right
   Just to try to make yourself more like her
   Or maybe to learn her behavior so well, you would be
   able to anticipate her next move before she could
   Lust, because that's what we really were
   Even though I dedicated hours convincing myself
   that it was more than smoke and mirrors

That we were the real deal like I thought we were
Greed, because sucking all the life out of me Robbing
me all of the trust I'd built up over a lifetime
Stealing my sense of security was never enough for you
Pride, for you were always too proud to admit you were a thief
Taking girls for granted, taking their innocence away from them
Wrath, for when you realized that when you stole
from me that you didn't do a full full sweep
And all of your malevolence boiled to the surface
You realized that you didn't snatch enough of my strength or
common sense for me to not flee the scene of the crime
Envy, for your misfortune in messing up once made you
jealous of those who executed their crimes without error

4. You kissed her but not like you kissed me
   With her, at least you could see in your hunch that
   you were already looking for the getaway car

5. You looked at me, and it almost set me back
   and made me fall a little again
   Almost

10 THINGS YOU NEED TO KNOW BEFORE DATING ME

1.) I love cats because I have nothing but respect for an
animal that adapted it's natural calling sound to mimic
one that sounds eerily similar to a human baby's cry
Just to ensure they are given attention

2.) I hate indecisive boys, because for christ's sake if I
have to pick where we eat every single time
We're going to have a problem

3.) I run a lot
Not because exercise is good for me, but because when i'm upset,
I'm either going to run, or write a poem about how I hate your guts
The choice is yours

4.) I love poetry, because while a picture is worth a thousand
words, no thousand year old picture will ever be able
to describe how wonderful you look right now

5.) I will love you more than a narcissist loves whoever invented mirrors
Care for you more than the sun cares for the green leaves
that only are green because of the sun's rays
And when you hurt me
I will swallow it and keep it down like a civil war soldier keeps
down liquor before having his arm sawed clean off

6.) My mother always comes first

7.) I liken myself to a cactus because while I can be a prick, I
require the most minimal of care to keep me flourishing

8.) I will have bad days in which I just will cry more
    tears than you ever thought possible.
    I will not drown
    And I will not become dehydrated
    Just give me love and I will be okay

9.) I prefer rainy days because the rain brings life to the
    gardens so they can exhibit colors so bright and display
    a show so eccentric, you'd think this wasn't real life

10.) I wrote this poem with you in mind, and I hope it doesn't bother you.
     I also hope these instructions will suffice to take care of me
     But I'll let you figure it out along the way.

A LETTER TO MY FUTURE DAUGHTER

Is today your birthday?
Is today the day you'll get your ears pierced? Is
today the day you'll learn to ride a bike?
I know you hear me, future daughter
Because you're part of me
So, I know you're always listening, even when you shouldn't
Because that's what I've always done

Let me start off by saying I love you Take note how
I haven't met you yet But I still love you
I don't know if you came from my belly or someone else's
I don't know if you'd rather be my son
I don't know if you'll be able to hear this when I read
it out loud or if I'll have to sign it to you
But I know that you're mine and that I love you

I don't know who your dad is yet, mon amour
But I know that he'll love you
And that he'll never leave
Because sweetheart, when my dad left
I had to turn from a seed to a tree really fast
I never got to enjoy being just a little sprout
I never got to enjoy growing up

Will you have siblings?
Oh honey, of course you will!
They might have different parents and different
colored skin and eyes and hair than you
But if you treat the whole world with kindness
Even when it tries to squeeze the last beat out of your heart

And drain all the blood from your veins that run like
trails throughout the beautiful forest that is you
You'll have family wherever you go
Just as long as you're kind before you're dismal

Speaking of blood
Your first period is going to be confusing
You're going to expect a flood of blood that rivals that of the amount of
blood that ran through the streets of Europe during the second World War
But it's going to be just enough to let you know
life is going to start moving pretty fast
And I hope that by the time that that rolls around
You'll have a boyfriend to tell you you're beautiful while you cry on his
chest because you saw a dog with a sweater on earlier that day
Or a girlfriend to sync up with so that you two can tell each other how
much you love each other while you eat all the food I have time to make

The world is going to seem cruel sometimes, my love
But it's because bad times have to hit you so
you can appreciate the good times
I'm always going to love you, honey
And I can't wait to meet you someday

A PERSONALITY CONUNNDRUM

Some people say they feel like Dr. Jekyll and Mr. Hyde
Living one life as a protector and another as a thief simultaneously
Their lives torn between the voice of an angel and the voice of a monster
A division between the two so thin that when they
are separated you don't even notice
And if you did notice the separation
Its because you got so close you got hurt
Mesmerized by Jekyll, and brutally murdered by Hyde

I, on the contrary, see myself more of a Marilyn
Monroe/Norma Jeane Mortenson
Seen either as one of the other while both inhabit the same body
And those who have seen both sides
Have gotten too close for safety
Gotten too close to not get cut by my diamonds
or shed the same red as my lipstick

I wake up in silk sheets and feel like Marilyn Monroe
Wanted for the satisfaction, needed for the physical Signing
my own name on papers, but never my child's
I held strange men in my arms because i could never hold my
own kin Sought after by those whose sheets are dirty from
the women before me Who just wanted to be famous
Just wanted to be beautiful
Just wanted to be adored
Bu instead ended up as a trophy on Hugh Hefner's wall
I mean, tricked into trading their passion for
entertaining others into faking passion for you
I mean, being desired
I put my lipstick on knowing where my lips have been

Whose bodies they've kissed
And how the bodies tell me that they love me and that i'm beautiful
And when i died
The same bodies showed up to my funeral
Stared at my body and wished that they could have gotten one last time in
How they could have saved me
But they never thought about how they loved me
Because they never really did

Other times, I go to bed thinking im Norma Jeane Mortenson
Who lives in her library surrounded by pages of simpler lives I'm
dying to live Finding the simple black and white comforting in
contrast to the blinding pinks and overwhelming reds that consume
me along with the emotions im paid to fake Because I can only act
like a damsel in distress so many times before becoming one Only
stand in front of a camera saying how ugly I am before I believe it
Only sing about heartbreak so many times before it becomes all I know
Only dance with my soul
With tears in my eyes
With memories of husbands past in my movements
My lonely nights in my swings and my dips Before i hate the body
that puts on the show And when I go home to my puppy
Knowing the dogs of men that follow me are long gone
I let a breath out like the eccentric fabric of my white dress
Relieved that the lights are cut and the rolling has stopped
Knowing my day is done and that i've only been Marilyn for part of my life
That I've always been Norma
That I'll always be me
In whatever form she comes

A TALE OF A TRAVELER'S WOE

I haven't come to a new land, but i yearn to breathe free
I walk through the front door of house unfamiliar to me
But has promised me a night where I forget my pain
Straightening my reliable grey v neck and making
sure my jean shorts were on just right

I manage to maneuver through the mass of people
Trying to find my place in the room
Trying to find my place in the world
But it seems as if it's not at the bottom of glasses
that held poisons I threw into my body
No matter how hard I looked, it just wasn't there

I heard a whistle in my mind at that moment, a train whistle to be exact
I'm not sure if it was a warning of danger, to get
off the tracks or a call to depart but
The whistle told me either way it was time to do something
Time to leave while the getting was good but I stayed and held my ground
With the hopes that this was just a bad feeling
Just a bad drink

The longer I stood in the living room The thicker the air
around me got The hazier my mind became
I thought maybe I saw the father of my future children across the room
But it was just another cloud
Just another smoke in the mirror trick

As I pushed through more people
Losing my fox-like kinesthetic intelligence
Becoming more like a lineman who has his
eyes shut and just knows to push
I feel the hand of a man I do not know lace around my arm
And the hand moves closer and closer to the place where
you can see what brand my jeans im wearing
I hear a boat horn
Warning either of dangerous waters or of a soon to come departure
But calling for me either way

As my feet lose their hold on the ground
And I see the stairs beneath me move and the man attached
to the unfamiliar hand carry me up the stairs
Away from the music
Away from the witnesses
Away from safety
I heard the beeping of the seatbelt sign on a plane
Because I knew, deep down,
I should've gotten out when i had the chance
I never should have gotten on the boat
I never should've started the car engine I never should have
came here tonight Because maybe if I would've stayed home
I could tell you what happened next and what
happened to my favorite grey tee shirt

ALL I COULD HOPE FOR

When I was in seventh grade
And my best friends were all getting boyfriends All i could hope for
was to be looked at Bespeckled, acne infested, and disproportionate
With the curves of my body that would one day be
as distinct as the peaks of the appalachians
Looking more like the remnants of a landslide at the time
Bumpy, with some areas raised more than others

When I got my first boyfriend
And all of my friends were out partying
All I could hope for was for this to be true love
Puppy love was fatal
Consuming and entrapping girls like flies
Leading them to believe love was like butterflies that made your head spin
That love wasn't more like a heron
Spreading its enormous wings and slicing
through the air with such momentum
It often time will destroy something
It often time will overwhelm you

When I met you
All I could hope for was that you would stay
My body and mind feeling more like a cheap motel
People coming and going with no regard for the state of the motel
No one wanting to do any housekeeping
Any maintenance
So the motel turns into roman ruins
A place of death, of destruction
A place haunted by warriors, champions of battles past
But now stands as a memorial Remembering those who died
as heros So the roman ruins turns into a battlefield
The home of flying bullets and the root of horrors soldiers relive everyday

Thinking their best friend who died next to him
Who he met in boot camp
Who loved his wife
Died because the corpse's best friend didn't fight hard enough
Didn't try hard enough
Wasn't enough

When I met him
All I could hope for was for you to be happy
The radio silence established upon our last kiss stopped
me from living a life i was so familiar with
One that was louder One that was brighter All I can hope for now
Is that you're doing okay

AN ODE TO FEMALES

An ode to bossy women
An ode to "sir, we closed ten minutes ago and i want to go home" women
An ode to "do you need something?" women

An ode to assertive women
Who don't settle for being paid less
Who use men's deodorant and razors because
they know they are cheaper and better
Who do not hush their voice to make a man more comfortable

An ode to confident women
Whose eyes send daggers into those who try to knock her down
Who send chills down the spine with the tone of voice
she uses when she tells you to get out of her face
Whose lips are perfectly straight and pulled so tight
It'll suffocate any breath taken with the intention of tearing her down

An ode to powerful women
Whose walk is so strong, it could lift an elephant
Who are so powerful, it could create an armistice
between Palestine and Israel
Who stand so tall
The tower of Pisa almost tripped her
The space station orbits her head like a halo

An ode to brilliant women
Who doubt themselves
But get up and smash glass ceilings like they're Jackie Robinson anyways
Who have you running in circles while she's barely jogging

An ode to women like you
Who in spite of the cruel people who tried to strip you of your
power And snatch your potential from the aura of success
that surrounds you And trip you up while you are making
strides toward starting a revolution An ode to you
Who in spite of everything Got here today Congratulations:
Keep silencing those who doubt you

AN ODE TO MIDWESTERN WOMEN

To the Donnas who can make a PTA meeting go silent when
she stands up and tells Sharon from across the room that she
was supposed to bring brownies next week, not this week:
I dedicate this to you
I write this in honor of midwestern women
Who will say "ope" as they pass you on the street

To the Kelly's and the Kaylia's who are going to "sneak right
pass you" Who will make a casserole out of anything
And are always maintaining traditions that were
established long before they were

To the rural Rachel's of Kansas City, Missouri
I salute you
Because while the winters are hard, the women are harder
When the going gets tough, the women of the midwest
do not flutter like snowflakes or flee for the border like the
Canadian geese that pepper the skies come November
No, midwest women toughen their exterior like the husks of corn
they grow everyday and feed every night to their families
Their families who they do everything to shield from danger
Who protect their daughters with pitchforks and hug
their sons so tight they turn into gravel roads
Roads that are known by the towns they live in by heart
And taken care of by the whole city

Praise to the Presleys that grow paisley
And endure small communities
Endure blazing summers and frigid winters
Endure all of the strenuous work of the farms they inhabit
And the suburbs they built with their bare hands
And after they built the cities with blood, sweat, and tears
They went and washed the dirt out from under their
nails and made corn casserole while singing
"Sweet Caroline"

A dedication to midwestern women
Who raised me
Because after all it, takes a village
Mine just happened to grow corn

AN ODE TO MY
BEST FRIEND

An ode to my best friend
Who's hair is so gorgeous
The beautiful stage of her body is curtained with blonde beauty after the
symphony of inside jokes and atrocious laughs finish their last encore

A poem for my best friend
Who will be a wonderful mother
But still scares me every time she gets behind the wheel
Blaring the music so loud, it seems like we at
least tried to cover our scream singing

A rambling of words for my best friend
Who's helped me cheat in school
But never helped me cheat myself out of self-care and self-love
Who's cheated off of me
But never fought me when I told her she was not a game to be cheated
She's not a joke to be laughed at
That she is royalty that needs to keep her head up
because I'm tired of picking up her crown after worthless
boys who try to take her power from her

A story about my best friend
Who's cried on my shoulder
Drowned me in her dreams, care, and tears
Who's so strong, she's carried me from places unknown
Dark places

Places where I shouldn't have been
Places I was too good for
To a place of happiness
A place of safety
A place formed by my best friend with my best interests in mind

A tale for my best friend And how she's beautiful And sees with her soul
Sees the tribulations everyone's been through And puts aside
everything's she has got to do To give everything she has to you
And how she loves with her entire being
Expresses anger in the sharp cracking of her knuckles
Shows disappointment in her silence
Exhibits happiness in the curling of her freckled nose
Tells her story in her walk
You can see her strength in her stride
Her resilience in her slight bounce of the heel

An ending for my best friend
And how she's my guardian angel And how i hope she
loves this poem As much as she loves me

AN ODE TO MY GRAMMY

An ode to my Grammy
Who is my Grammy, not my Grandma, Because
"Grandma" makes her feel old

My Grammy stands at 4"8" On a good day
And takes me to the store with her to get things off of shelves for her
But will scare you half to death if you talk to her the wrong way

My Grammy is so sweet, She'd melt your heart on sight
And maybe give you a couple cavities too

My Grammy
who loves me most
My Grammy
Who has a picture of me flicking off the white house standing proudly in
front of the picture of her other granddaughter on a mission trip in India
Because she loves my spunk

My Grammy
Who never thinks you ate enough

My Grammy
Who is so smart
She tricked me into going to church
And I think God is as real as the tooth fairy

My Grammy
Who came from nothing
Who came from an alcoholic father like my own
But scratched and clawed to have the perfect life she always wanted

And smiled through every hardship
Every heartbreak
And cleared every hurdle that was in her path with ease

My Grammy
Who is so stupid crazy, German stubborn
She took a DNA test to make sure "VonEpp" was really German
And feeds all the neighborhood cats because she can't
stand the thought of any creature going hungry
And put cat butt magnets over all pictures of my dad on family
pictures on the fridge after he left us because "Assholes should
always be seen as assholes and never treated any better"
And drove 2 and a half hours to see me for 10 minutes,
Even though she has to sit on three phonebooks
to see over the steering wheel\

Ode to my Grammy
Who told me:
"Great women deserve beautiful flowers" Who told me:
"Love loudly, or not at all" Who told me:
"Cook well, or just order out and put it on plates before
anyone sees it—no one will know the difference"
Who told me:
"Don't lose your voice, sometimes it's all you got"

AN OPEN LETTER TO TEENAGE BOYS

If I went to Harvard
Got a degree in neuroscience
Got another degree in behavioral science
And did my graduate work in abnormal psychology
And had to pick subjects to study
I'd pick you every time
Because the male species from ages 13-20 is
one that is not human nor animal
But some sort of alien in between

The half-man, half-beast species dedicates years
of practice desensitizing themself to smell
A man must have no weakness
Therefore, by leaving mountains of towels on
the ground for months at a time
Stacking up on top of each other like a 12 car pile up
You learn to embrace the swamp you've began to inhabit
Much like Shrek, Yoda, or any form of mold
Making you not only immune to all smells but also
immune to common sense and personal hygiene

The male creature also takes much pride in their fur
The fur upon their head most usually is sprinkled
with white specks of dandruff
Or so you thought
In reality, the white specks were strategically placed by the
creature himself as a form of protection against the she-beast
For the white specks are actually laced crystal deposits
Blessed by an ancient shaman to banish the woman
monster away from the he-creature's presence

The subhuman species is also a clan of fearless warriors
Dedicating half their time to perfecting their war face
Ensuring all 3 hairs on their left cheek, 2 hairs on their right cheek,
and 5 hairs on the tip on their chin are prominently showing
And the other half of their ever-so precious time preparing
for battle with the unslayable female creature
Thousands of years have been dedicated to studying their weaknesses,
but to no avail! The she-beast can take a razor-sharp blade
Drag it against various surfaces of her body
And survive
The femme-monster has learned to drain
herself of all it's blood once a month
Just to ensure they never really die
The half-woman, half-stalker-in-the-night can also
change the color of it's fur at the drop of a pin!
It could be blue, black, brown, blonde, pink, or purple
With thick, long fur glistening so valiantly in the sun's rays
Or short, thin fur to signify it's fearlessness
The part girl, part god species also can wear weapons on their
feet Making sure to carry knives on their heels everywhere they
go Showing how truly war-ready they are at any given time
They also carry knives in the gems that sit in their skull
Shooting looks so fatally sharp
It could make any man monster run for the motherland

Poor, poor male species
I close with this:
The nation's top scientists and I will be working
diligently and watching closely
For those 7 years of struggle is a mystery that's still unsolved

COMFORT LIES

I sit at the end of the couch and the boy holds my hand
I look down and notice the scars on my arm that came from when
I fought my loneliest nights I see the craters between my fingers
in which my tears run down and ater the valley of my palms
The boy looks me in the eyes and tells me he loves me and I believe him
He's broken me once
He's broken so many girls behind me
Leaving a trail of tears that only carries his name on
the backs of those forced to walk this path
We, the women slaine by the boy, how good of a
poker player he'd be while we march
Keeping his eyes on us, but on other players too
Never focusing on what is immediately in front of him
But I believe him and tell him I love him too because I do
I love the slime slathered boy who can't afford
to be caught in any woman's hands
Just falls gracefully from one palm valley to the next
As my raindrops do

The man shows me his new house and tells me everything
is only going to get better from here and I believe him
In spite of the fact that I have every reason not to
Why should I trust the man who had 21 years to love the
first family he had but went out and had another?
Have faith in the man who I had to take care of when he was too riddled
with alcohol to distinguish between his daughter and another bottle?
Attempting to pour my innocence and independence straight out of me?
Believe the man who once spent his few nights home singing "Hey
Jude" to me, not knowing John Lennon wrote the ballad for his son
when he was leaving his wife and son in an attempt to comfort him?
I believe the man anyways

Because I want the man who own the same emerald eyes and pronounce
Roman nose to see his first daughter as the one he loves most

The woman whose hair dreads like mine and cries
only at night tells me she's not tired and I
believed her
I want the woman to go to bed
She's tired from pushing two children all alone
with no one to drag her along
From wasting 30 years on a marriage that she kept vows for
From working 3 jobs to pay rent
I want the woman to dream
Dream of a world where she doesn't have to push the children
That the home is paid for and her laboring and suffering is over
She does not have to break her back one vertebrae at a
time for her right to live anymore in this dreamland
I kiss the woman on her worn, leathery cheek and tell
her I'll be home in an hour and that I love her
And I sit in my car and cry for 20 minutes because
I can't build the dreamland for the woman
I can only try to buy her a plane ticket to the dreamland

I don't want to write about the boy who has eyes for others
The father who left
The mother who slaves
But heartbreak makes the best material and by god, is my heart broken
It's been thrown into a deli slicer
Slathered on to some sub par sandwich
Devoured by a man who won't let his wife see the
light of day without seeing his belt first

Sent through his gastrointestinal tract, to the toilet, and
eventually to the ocean where my last remains of my
heart gets chowed upon by some bottom feeder
I write so those whose hearts have sent through wood chippers
Garbage disposals
Shredders
Mincer and weedwackers know they aren't alone

I finish this work and tell myself i'll start writing happier work
But happiness isn't a two page poem
I know this to be a fact
I believe myself anyways

DEAD THINGS

I didn't know I was in a cemetery
I didn't know corpses could talk since people who are dead to me
Keep trying to speak to me

I didn't know this was a grave
Because I keep trying to bury the hatchet and memories of you
And you still just want to suffocate my dreams

I didn't know this was a funeral
Because I'm trying to pay homage to the parts of me you killed
The good girl you shot for sport
The honest girl turned criminal who went down in a shootout in
a parking lot when she told you she couldn't do this anymore
Couldn't love you anymore Couldn't breathe anymore
Couldn't function anymore And here you are,
Staring into the casket, Not shedding a tear

I didn't know this was a seance
Because you're haunting me from my past life

HABITS

Much like a zookeeper looking after a frail bird
Or a librarian looking over books who's message
surpass their publishing dates
I've fallen into habits
Little ticks, miniscule routines, daily systems that are carried out
In order to make sure that nothing is disturbed or out of place

I've learned to tiptoe up and down the stairs
To weave and maneuver in order to avoid making a sound
To avoid making my presence known in my own house
Because if you woke Daddy up from his sleep
After he works nights and days for another family
that we know of but don't speak about
He would make sure you didn't make a sound

I've learned to keep my face low when speaking to men
For I can only stifle my voice so much
Only balance between "speaking up" and "knowing my place" so much
That hanging my face towards the floor seems
to suppress the sound the most
Because good boys don't like loud girls
Good boys don't like girls who speak up for themselves
So you got to keep quiet, you got to keep to yourself
If you want a good boy to silence your voice as long as he's around

I've learned to be an artist
And get up at the crack at dawn to paint my face, and get into a costume
To make sure I don't have too much skin, too much makeup
But just enough to show that I'm trying to impress everyone except myself
Put on a fake face for everyone except myself

Put on a show for everyone except myself
Because pretty girls can't be confident in themselves
Beautiful women have to come with photoshop and
surgery scars from fillings and removals
So, you better fake it until you make it

But I wasn't born with a fire in my belly
A war call in my vocal chords
A walk so strong it wakes the devil up when I hit the floor in the morning
And a face so perfectly formed with the best parts of
the women before me with the same last name
The same DNA
The same habits from those who wanted to turn us into shadows
Silent and unnoticed unless intentionally looked for
To sit here and continue the family traditions
Because like my mama said, all bad habits must at one point be broken

/